Carolin Kotthaus

Soul Food in Langston Hughes' "Simple's Uncle Sam"

GRIN Verlag

Bibliografische Information der Deutschen Nationalbibliothek:

Die Deutsche Bibliothek verzeichnet diese Publikation in der Deutschen National-
bibliografie; detaillierte bibliografische Daten sind im Internet über http://dnb.d-
nb.de/ abrufbar.

Imprint:

Copyright © 2010 GRIN Verlag GmbH
Druck und Bindung: Books on Demand GmbH, Norderstedt Germany
ISBN: 978-3-656-46159-3

This book at GRIN:

http://www.grin.com/en/e-book/230108/soul-food-in-langston-hughes-simple-s-
uncle-sam

GRIN - Your knowledge has value

Der GRIN Verlag publiziert seit 1998 wissenschaftliche Arbeiten von Studenten, Hochschullehrern und anderen Akademikern als eBook und gedrucktes Buch. Die Verlagswebsite www.grin.com ist die ideale Plattform zur Veröffentlichung von Hausarbeiten, Abschlussarbeiten, wissenschaftlichen Aufsätzen, Dissertationen und Fachbüchern.

Visit us on the internet:

http://www.grin.com/

http://www.facebook.com/grincom

http://www.twitter.com/grin_com

Bergische Universität Wuppertal

Anglistik

WS 09/10

As American as Apple Pie

Langston Hughes – Simple's Uncle Sam

BA

3. Semester

Table of contents

1.   Introduction

This paper is going to deal with the poet and author Langston Hughes and his stories published under the title *Simple's Uncle Sam* during the era of Modernism and Postmodernism.

I am going to begin with a short biographical overview about Langston Hughes' life. The information used, is taken from the Wikipedia website entry about Langston Hughes (en.wikipedia.org) but can also be found on more reliable websites (poemhunter.com; nathanielturner.com).

Since this paper is part of the course 'As American as Apple Pie' which is concerned with the meaning of food scenes in different texts, I will present the topic of 'soul food'. I am going to explain where soul food has its roots and what it exactly is.

Further I am going to show what important role soul food or food in general plays in the extracts of *Simple's Uncle Sam* and how it refers to the ethnical and cultural background of African Americans.

2.   A short biographical overview of Langston Hughes' life

Langston Hughes was born as James Mercer Langston Hughes on February 1, 1902 in Joplin, Missouri and died at the age of 65 on May 22, 1967 in New York City.

He was an citizen of the United States of America with parents who were both mixed raced being descendants of African Americans, European Americans and Native Americans.

Born into a politically very active family, he was raised with a sense of racial pride to be a Black American.

In high school, he discovered his love for books and he began writing short texts.

Attending the Lincolns University in Pennsylvania afterwards, which is known to be a historically black university, he got a Bachelor degree in 1929.

Most time of his life he was an author, having his writing period to have taken place from 1926 to 1964.

He moved to Harlem, New York and became known as a famous writer of the Harlem Renaissance and as one of the earliest innovators of the new literary art form of jazz poetry. Concentrating his poetry and fiction generally on views of the working class lives of African Americans in the United States, he presented a certain pride of African American identity and spoke out for keeping this pride instead of assimilating to the norms of White Americans.

During his writing period and also after his death many black writers considered his writings.

3.   Simple's Uncle Sam

During his writing period, Langston Hughes wrote several books (for example: *Simple Speaks His Mind*, 1950; *Simple Takes a Wife*, 1953; *Simple Stakes a Claim*, 1957; *Simple's Uncle Sam*, 1965) that had a main character named Mr. Jesse Semple or, as a nickname, Simple who is an African American.

This character was supposed to be the voice of African Americans during the Jim Crow era while racial segregation was widely discussed.

Since the figure 'Uncle Sam' is a symbol for the United States, the title *Simple's Uncle Sam* points to a certain view how the character Simple looks upon the USA.

The contexts of these little stories are the civil rights movements of the 1950s and 1060s.

4.   Soul Food

Soul food is a certain kind of food with special ingredients and seasonings relating to the African American culture with a main stress on the southern states of the USA.

4.1.   Historical background

The origins of soul food are to be found in times of slavery in the United States. The black slaves got for food just the unwanted and cheap groceries, often those ones which the white masters didn't like.

This image of soul food, to be a food of the slaves or afterwards one of the discriminated Blacks, changed during the 1960s. Soul food became a part of the ethnic identity of Black US-Americans and special soul food restaurants were opened. Soul food began to be something fashionable and to be not just for the African Americans any more.

4.2.   Ingredients

Since the groceries had to be cheap, the slaves used what they could get, for example pig feet, chitterlings, chicken liver, black-eyed peas or collard greens. They used a lot of fat and salt to make these ingredients tasty so that soul food is known to be a very heavy, fatty kind of food.

Contrary to the background of the African Americans, soul food does not consist just of an African cuisine which uses the seasoning okra. In fact, it is also influenced by European and Native American cooking. Corn pudding is an example, since the corn is an ingredient of the Native American cuisine.

5.   (Soul) food in the stories of *Simple's Uncle Sam*

The chapters from the book *Simple's Uncle Sam* which were important for the course are *Empty Houses, Haircuts and Paris, Swinging High* and *Soul Food*. Every chapter has its own scenes wherein food, especially soul food, plays an important role.

5.1.   Empty Houses

This chapter is concerned with ice cream, beer and (Sunday) dinner.

Simple tells from his childhood. He tells how he was a little boy and a white man gave him ice cream on a hot day. When he came home and reported that he got an ice cream cone for free from a white man his relatives did not believe him and punished him for lying. They cannot imagine a white man who gives a little black boy something for free. Here one can see the thoughts of the African Americans of this time which are still influenced by the impressions of slavery. They do not believe that there are white people who do something without wanting something back.

Simple in contrast does believe it and he does not "hate all white folks" (Hughes, 12). For him this balance of life (cf. Hughes, 13) – receiving and giving back – is not necessary; he is willing to give without demanding for something else. He uses the beer someone gives him as an example that life can function without this balance if the gift "comes from the heart" (Hughes, 13).

Although he does not hate every white man, he does not feel excepted in the white man's world either. He was raised in a white system wherein even the bible cards showed a white Jesus (cf. Hughes, 14). He talks about the loneliness of a (Sunday) dinner if there is no one who welcomes you and says "You're mine" (Hughes, 15). The food can be as good as possible but if there is no one he belongs to, it is worth nothing.

5.2.   Haircuts and Paris

Simple talks about the only reason he would come back for if he moved to Paris. This reason is the soul food which he describes as "corn bread and pigs' feet and greens" (Hughes, 64). One can see why Simple would like to live in Paris. There, he could feel being accepted what is impossible for him in the USA. He says that in the States, the white man still has the "whip hand" (Hughes, 63) which relates to the times of slavery when the whites masters whipped their slaves. In the States, African American men cannot feel like real men because they need to go to colored barbershops, restaurants, hospitals and even to colored undertakers (cf. Hughes, 63). This kind of sarcastic talking shows the discontentment of the African Americans. The only roots they have in the USA can be seen in the soul food which also relates back to slavery.

5.3.   Soul Food

In the beginning, Simple talks about Harlem. This is remarkable because the author Langston Hughes himself lived there. Simple explains that "thirty years ago Harlem was blooming" (Hughes, 110). This time is known as the Harlem Renaissance when many poets and artists lived and worked there. The Harlem existing now is not the same anymore; it is just famous for the politician and civil rights leader Adam Powell (cf. Hughes, 110). Further, Simple talks about integration and tells a story of an old lady who wanted to test if the white people are actually ready for integration (cf. Hughes, 113). She goes to a white restaurant and tries to order different soul food meals like "collard greens and ham hocks", "black-eyed peas and pig tails" or "chitterlings" (Hughes, 113). She learns that not a single of these meals can be served in that restaurant what makes her say that the white people are not "ready for integration" (Hughes, 113) yet. Simple adds that this was an American restaurant and they still didn't have soul food cf. Hughes, 114). The striking thing about this scene is that the old lady and Simple think of integration in the opposite way than the Whites do. The term integration how the White Americans interpret it is that the African Americans need to fit in the White American culture but for the old lady and Simple integration means that the Whites need to accept and integrate into the African American system. The old lady feels already as a part of the USA and sees a need for the Whites to change their habits. For Simple soul food is a part of America and of American history just as everything else what the White Americans think of to be a part of it. Here one can see

6

Langston Hughes concept of feeling proud to be an African American instead of assimilating to the norms of the Whites.

Further, Simple talks about restaurants which try to cook soul food but fail because they do it in a wrong way. He says that pork chop, chicken or fish must be fresh (cf. Hughes, 114). This quote represents the opinion of African American people from that time. There were even books written for a white female audience to learn what soul food actually is and how it is cooked in a correct way. It should not be "frozen" or "cooked […] for three hours" (Witt, 233)

5.4. Swinging High

The chapter starts with Simple criticizing foreign names for familiar food. He gives an example of a meal called 'BOLA-BOLAS' which sounds very foreign and interesting and actually consists just of meatballs (cf. Hughes, 4). Simple prefers the well-known soul food, the "plain old down-home victuals" (Hughes, 4) instead of anything foreign, even if it is modern to eat foreign food. For him, soul food shows his relation to the south of the USA and of his roots.

He is asked how he likes a certain modern negro-owned restaurant and Simple even criticizes this one because he does not like the wide range of meals one can order. He likes it as simple as possible and just wants "pork chops, bread and gravy" (Hughes, 5). The offered meals, which are "chicken stewed in curry sauce" (Hughes, 4), "rice pudding" or "olives" (Hughes, 5), belong to people of the high society according to Simple. He does not like these fancy things.

The only thing he would add to his meal are "fried apples" (Hughes, 5) because those remind him of his childhood when he used to swing on a rope attached to an apple tree in his uncle's garden (cf. Hughes, 5). The swing reminds him of life; he compares the swinging with living and means that life is hard if one is colored; one needs a "stout hard" and one needs to "pump hard" (Hughes, 6) to achieve something in life.

6.   Conclusion

As all these scenes have shown, soul food is an important term in Langston Hughes' stories *Simple's Uncle Sam*. It represents roots, pride and life of African Americans in the United States.

Some utterances of Simple seem to fit to his nickname but if one looks more deeply one sees that these utterances are not simple at all but wisely spoken to present a certain look on the USA from an African American's point of view which differs from the opinions and utterances of White Americans. Often one can read between the lines and see Langston Hughes' attempts to inform his audience about historical and cultural background and political opinions of African Americans.

References

"Biography of Langston Hughes." <http://www.poemhunter.com/langston-hughes/biography/> (March 2, 2010)

Hughes, Langston. "Empty Houses." Simple's Uncle Sam. New York: Hill and Wang, 1965. 12-16.

Hughes, Langston. "Haircuts in Paris." Simple's Uncle Sam. New York: Hill and Wang, 1965. 63-65

Hughes, Langston. "Soul Food." Simple's Uncle Sam. New York: Hill and Wang, 1965. 110-18.

Hughes, Langston. "Swinging High." Simple's Uncle Sam. New York: Hill and Wang, 1965. 4-8.

"Langston Hughes." ChickenBones: Journal for Literary & Artistic African-American Themes. <http://www.nathanielturner.com/langstonhughesbio.htm> (March 2, 2010)

"Langston Hughes." Wikipedia. <http://en.wikipedia.org/wiki/Langston_Hughes> (March 2, 2010)

Witt, Doris. "'My Kitchen Was the World': Vertemae Smart Grosvenor's Geechee Diaspora." Kitchen Culture in America: Popular Representations of Food, Gender, and Race. Ed. Sherrie A. Inness. Philadelphia: University of Pennsylvania Press, 2001. 233